The Silly Little Book

of

ANIMAL JOKES

The Silly Little Book
of
ANIMAL
JOKES

This is a Parragon Book

This edition published in 2000

Parragon
Queen Street House
4 Queen Street
Bath BA1 1HE, UK

Produced by Magpie Books, an imprint of
Robinson Publishing Ltd, London

ISBN 0-75253-688-5

A copy of the British Library Cataloguing-in-Publication Data
is available from the British Library

Printed and bound in Singapore

Contents

Introduction

Roaming the pages of this terrific Noah's Ark of jokes is a menagerie of animals, bugs and slimy things, from the mosquito on holiday (he was an itch-hiker) to the elephant who sat on a grape (it let out a little wine). There are enough gags and funny stories in here to keep you roaring with laughter and hooting with delight for months to come.

Birds

What's the difference between a
fly and a bird?
A bird can fly but a fly can't bird.

Why did the sparrow fly into the
library?
It was looking for bookworms.

What do you call a snake that is
trying to become a bird?
A feather boa.

What do two lovesick owls say
when it's raining?
Too-wet-to-woo!

What sits in a tree and says,
"Hoots, mon. Hoots, mon?"
A Scottish owl.

Why were the mommy and daddy
owls worried about their son?
Because he didn't seem to give a
hoot anymore.

What does an educated owl say?
Whom.

Why did the owl 'owl?
Because the Woodpecker would
peck 'er.

What do confused owls say?
Too-whit-to-why?

What did the owl say to his friend
as he flew off?
Owl be seeing you later.

What did the baby owl's parents
say when he wanted to go to a
party?
You're not owld enough.

What did the owls do when one of
them had a punk haircut?
They hooted with laughter.

What do Scottish owls sing?
Owld Lang Syne.

What did the scornful owl say?
Twit twoo.

How do you know that owls are
cleverer than chickens?
Have you ever heard of Kentucky
Fried Owl?

What do you get if you cross King Kong with a budgie?
A messy cage.

What do you get if you cross an owl with a witch?
A bird that's ugly but doesn't give a hoot.

How do you know you are haunted by a parrot?
He keeps saying, "oooo's a pretty boy then?"

1st man: My wife eats like a bird.

2nd man: You mean she hardly eats a thing?

1st man: No, she eats slugs and worms.

Knock, knock.
Who's there?
Owl.
Owl who?
Owl I can say is "Knock, knock!"

Knock, knock.
Who's there?
Owl.
Owl who?
Owl be sad if you don't let me in.

Knock, knock.
Who's there?
Owl.
Owl who?
Owl aboard!

Knock, knock.
Who's there?
Baby Owl.
Baby Owl who?
Baby Owl see you later, baby not.

Two owls were playing pool.
One said, "Two hits."
The other replied, "Two hits to who?"

Why did the vulture cross the road?
For a fowl reason.

Why don't vultures fly south in the winter?
Because they can't afford the air fare.

Why did a man's pet vulture not make a sound for five years?
It was stuffed.

What do you call a team of vultures playing football?
Fowl play.

Where do vultures meet for coffee?
In a nest-cafe.

Where do the toughest vultures
come from?
Hard-boiled eggs.

What do you call a vulture with no
beak?
A head-banger.

Why couldn't the vulture talk to the
dove?
Because he didn't speak pidgin
English.

How do we know vultures are religious?
Because they're birds of prey.

What do a vulture, a pelican and a taxman have in common?
Big bills!

What happened when a doctor crossed a parrot with a vampire?
It bit his neck, sucked his blood and said, "Who's a pretty boy, then?"

A woodpecker was pecking a hole in a tree. All of a sudden a flash of lightning struck the tree to the ground. The woodpecker looked bemused for a moment and then said: "Gee, I guess I don't know my own strength."

Why does a stork stand on one leg?
Because it would fall over if it lifted the other one.

Teacher: Who can tell me what geese eat?
Paul: Er, gooseberries, Sir?

Dave: The trouble with our teachers is that they all do bird impressions.
Mave: Really? What do they do?
Dave: They watch us like hawks.

Doctor, doctor, my wife thinks she's a duck.
You better bring her in to see me straight away.
I can't do that – she's already flown south for the winter.

A monster decided to become a TV star, so he went to see an agent.
"What do you do?" asked the agent.
"Bird impressions," said the monster.
"What kind of bird impressions?"
"I eat worms."

Which bird is always out of breath?
A puffin.

What's the difference between a gymnastics teacher and a duck?
One goes quick on its legs, the other goes quack on its legs.

Did you hear about the village idiot buying bird seed?
He said he wanted to grow some birds.

Teacher, in pet shop: I'd like to buy a budgie, please. How much do they cost?

Pet shop owner: $10 apiece.

Teacher, horrified: How much does a whole one cost?

Teacher: What's a robin?

John: A bird that steals, Miss.

Donald: My canary died of flu.

Dora: I didn't know canaries got flu.

Donald: Mine flew into a car.

Teacher: Why do birds fly south in winter?

Jim: Because it's too far to walk.

Bugs and
Spiders

What is a termite's favorite
breakfast?
Oak-meal.

What did one termite say to the
other termite when he saw a house
burning?
Barbecue tonight!

What do you call an amorous
insect?
The Love Bug.

What do you call an insect that has just flown by?
A flu bug.

What did the termite say in the pub?
Is the bar tender here?

What did the termite say when he saw that his friends had completely eaten a chair?
Wooden you know it!

How do you keep flies out of the kitchen?
Put a bucket of manure in the lounge.

Which fly makes films?
Stephen Spielbug.

Which fly captured the ladybird?
The dragon-fly.

Why did the firefly keep stealing things?
He was light-fingered.

What goes snap, crackle, pop?
A firefly with a short circuit.

How do fireflies start a race?
Ready, steady, glow!

What did one firefly say to another?
Got to glow now.

If there are five flies in the kitchen, which one is the American football player?
The one in the sugar bowl.

Why were the flies playing football in a saucer?
They were playing for the cup.

Waiter, I must say that I don't like all the flies in this dining room! Tell me which ones you don't like and I'll chase them out for you.

A little firefly was in school one day and he put up his hand.

"Please, miss, may I be excused?"

"Yes," replied the teacher, "when you've got to glow, you've got to glow."

How do you know if you have a
tough mosquito?
If you slap him, he slaps you back.

What has six legs, bites and talks
in code?
A morse-quito.

What's the difference between a
mosquito and a fly?
Try sewing buttons on a mosquito!

What's the difference between a lawyer and a mosquito?
A mosquito drops off you when you die.

Why is it best to be bitten quickly by one mosquito?
Because an itch in time saves nine.

Which is the most religious insect in the Middle East?
A mosque-ito.

What is small and grey, sucks
blood and eats cheese?
A mouse-quito.

Why did the mosquito go to the
dentist?
To improve his bite.

What wears a black cape, flies
through the night and sucks
blood?
A mosquito in a cape.

Why are mosquitoes religious?
They prey on you.

Why are mosquitoes annoying?
Because they get under your skin.

What do you get if you cross a
mosquito with a knight?
A bite in shining armor.

What's the mosquitoes' favorite song?
I've Got You Under My Skin.

What do you call A Tale of Two Mosquitoes?
A bite-time story.

What did one mosquito say to another when they came out of the theater?
Fancy a bite?

What is a mosquito's favorite
sport?
Skin-diving.

What's the name of the opera
about a mouse and a flea?
Die Fleadermouse.

What did one amorous flea say to
the other?
I love you aw-flea.

What is the insect family's favorite
game?
Cricket.

Why do we know that insects have
amazing brains?
Because they always know when
you're having a picnic.

What lives in gum trees?
Stick insects.

What is the best insect chat-up line?
Pardon me, but is this stool taken?

What happened to the man who turned into an insect?
He beetled off.

Moths – when will they learn that if a light is bright, then it probably isn't the moon?
And when it's my head, they're smacking into then they'll soon meet a rolled-up newspaper.

Daddy Long Legs: Oh look, a human, someone far bigger than I am. I know, I'll fly into them until I've annoyed them enough to kill me, then I'll do it some more until they've completed their mission.

Bees – shouldn't someone tell them that they'll die if they sting you?

Spiders – these are the animals that find their way into your bath, and then stay there. Why don't they get it into their heads that the bath is the last place they should explore?

Wasps – while everyone runs a mile when they see one, why does it take hours for them to work out how to get out of a room, even after you've opened the window that they're standing on?

Ants – so, they can carry ten times their own body weight! Thousands of years on this planet and they still haven't worked out how to build a truck!

Bluebottles – what is the point of their existence?
Don't they realise that if they insist on buzzing round your bedroom when you're trying to get some sleep that any minute now they'll have their buzzing stopped forever?

Snails – get an engine or something!

What do you call a nervous insect?
Jitterbug.

Who stole the sheets off the bed?
Bed buglars.

What do you call a top pop group
made up of nits?
The Lice Girls.

What car do insects drive?
A Volkswagen Beetle.

What do you say to an annoying
cockroach?
Stop bugging me!

What insect can fly underwater?
A bluebottle in a submarine.

What do you call an insect from outer space?
Bug Rogers.

What's the grasshoppers' favorite band?
Buddy Holly and the Crickets.

What do you get if you cross a praying mantis with a termite?
A bug that says grace before eating your house.

What did one stick insect say to another?
Stick around.

Why is the letter "t" so important to a stick insect?
Without it, it would be a sick insect.

What do you call a mayfly with a machine gun?
Baddy Long Legs.

What creepie crawlies do athletes break?
Tapeworms.

Why did the termite eat a sofa and two chairs?
It had a suite tooth.

How do you get rid of termites?
Exterminite them.

What lies down a hundred feet in the air?
A centipede.

What kind of insects live on the moon?
Lunar ticks.

46

What's the difference between head lice and nits?
A real nit is too stupid to find your head.

What's the difference between a maggot and a cockroach?
Cockroaches crunch more when you eat them.

How do insects travel when they go on holiday?
They go for a buggy ride.

Why was the insect kicked out of the park?
It was a litterbug.

What do you call singing insects?
Humbugs.

What is the insects' favorite pop group?
The Beatles.

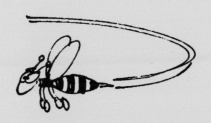

What do you call a mosquito on holiday?
An itch-hiker.

What do you get if you cross the Lone Ranger with an insect?
The Masked-quito.

What has antlers and sucks your blood?
A moose-quito.

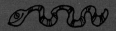

What do insects learn at school?
Mothematics.

What insect lives on nothing?
A moth, because it eats holes.

How can you make a moth ball?
Hit it with a fly swatter.

Where do butterflies hire their
dinner jackets?
Moth Bros.

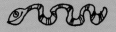

What is pretty and delicate and
carries a sub-machine gun?
A killer butterfly.

How do you make a butterfly?
Flick it out of the dish with a
butter knife.

What do you get if you cross a
moth with a firefly?
An insect that can find its way
around a dark wardrobe.

How do stones stop moths eating
your clothes?
Because a rolling stone gathers no
moths.

What is a myth?
A female moth.

Why did the moth nibble a hole in
the carpet?
He wanted to see the floor show.

Who do all moths bow to?
The Moth-er Superior.

Why was the moth so unpopular?
He kept picking holes in
everything.

What likes to spend the summer in
a fur coat and the winter in a
swim-suit?
A moth.

Why wouldn't they let the butterfly
into the dance?
Because it was a moth ball.

Why did the butterfly?
Because it saw the milk-float.

What circles the lampshade at 200 mph?
Stirling Moth.

What is the biggest moth?
A mam-moth.

What do bees do if they want to use public transport?
Wait at a buzz stop.

What's an English bee's favorite TV station?
The Bee-Bee C.

What does a queen bee do when she belches?
She issues a royal pardon.

How does a queen bee get around
the hive?
She's throne.

What's yellow and brown and
covered in blackberries?
A bramble bee.

What is more dangerous than
being with a fool?
Fooling with a bee.

Why did the bee start spouting poetry?
It was waxing lyrical.

Who is the bees' favorite composer?
Bee-thoven.

What did the mommy bee say to the naughty little bee?
Bee-hive yourself!

Can bees fly in the rain?
Not without their little yellow jackets.

What goes hum-choo, hum-choo?
A bee with a cold.

What is a bee-line?
The shortest distance between two buzz-stops.

What's the difference between a very old, shaggy Yeti and a dead bee?
One's a seedy beast and the other's a deceased bee.

Who wrote books for little bees?
Bee-trix Potter.

What do you call a bee who's had a spell put on him?
Bee-witched.

What has brown and yellow stripes
and buzzes along at the bottom of
the sea?
A bee in a submarine.

Why do bees hum?
Because they've forgotten the
words.

What kind of bee hums and drops
things?
A fumble bee.

What did the bee say to the flower?
Hello, honey.

What are the bees' favorite flowers?
Bee-gonias

What is brown and yellow and buzzes at 36,000 feet in the air?
A bee in an airplane.

What did the confused bee say?
To bee or not to bee.

What are the cleverest bees?
Spelling bees.

Which bee is good for your health?
Vitamin bee.

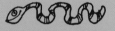

What goes zzub, zzub?
A bee flying backwards.

Why do bees buzz?
They can't whistle.

Why did the bee have its legs
crossed as it flew?
It was looking for the BP station.

What bee can never be
understood?
A mumble-bee.

What do you get if you cross a bee
with a quarter of a pound of
minced beef?
A humburger.

Who is a bee's favorite painter?
Pablo Beecasso.

What is a baby bee?
A little humbug.

What is the bees' favorite film?
The Sting.

What did the mommy bee say to
her naughty son?
Just beehive!

What did the drone say to the
Queen Bee?
Swarm in here, isn't it?

Who's top of the charts in the beehive?
Sting.

What did the spider say to the bee?
Your honey or your life.

Where do bees keep their money?
In a honey-box.

Which is the bees' favorite pop group?
The Bee Gees.

What is the bees' favorite TV channel?
The Bee Bee C.

What is the bees' favorite novel?
The Great Gats-bee.

What do you get if you cross a bee
with a door-bell?
A hum-dinger.

How many bees do you need in a
proper bee choir?
A humdred.

What does the bee Santa Claus
say at Christmas?
Ho-hum-hum.

Why did the bees go on strike?
Because they wanted more honey
and shorter working flowers.

Why do bees have sticky hair?
Because of the honey combs.

Where do bees come from?
Stingapore.

What kind of gum do bees chew?
Bumble-gum.

Which queen can never wear a
crown?
A queen bee.

Why did the queen bee kick all the
other bees out of the hive?
Because they kept droning on and
on.

What does a bee say before it stings you?
This is going to hurt me much more than it hurts you.

What do you call a bee that can shelter a plane?
An aero-drone.

If bees make honey, what do wasps make?
Waspberry jam.

Where do you take a sick wasp?
To waspital.

What is the wasps' favorite song?
Just a Spoonful of Sugar.

What did the bee say to the wasp
who tried to make honey?
Don't wasp your time!

Insect Films: The Fly; Batman; Beetlejuice; The Sting; The Good, the Bug and the Ugly; The Frog Prince; Four Webbings and a Funeral; Seven Bats for Seven Brothers.

What's the difference between a monster orangutan and a flea? A monster orangutan can have a flea but a flea can't have a monster orangutan.

What do you get if you cross a witch with a flea?
Very worried dogs.

Collecting Mosquitoes – by Lara Bites

Collecting Mosquitoes – by Ethan Alive

While visiting close friends, a gnat,
Decided to sleep in a hat.
But an elderly guest
Decided to rest
Now the gnat and the hat are
quite flat.

A fly and a flea in a flue
Were wondering what they should
do.
Said the fly, "Let us flee!" Said
the flea, "Let us fly."
So they flew, through a flaw in the
flue.

I say, I say, I say. What has a purple-spotted body, ten hairy legs and eyes on stalks?
I don't know.
Nor do I, but there's one creeping up your back!

Girl: Can you eat spiders?
Boy: Why?
Girl: One's just crawled into your sandwich.

Bluebottle: I must fly.
Bee: OK, I'll give you a buzz later.

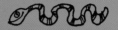

Boy: Mom, mom, I've just
swallowed a spider.
Mom: Shall I get the doctor to give
you something for it?
Boy: No, let it starve to death.

Boy: Dad, dad, there's a spider in the bath.

Dad: What wrong with that? You've seen spiders before.

Boy: Yes, but this one is three feet wide and using all the hot water!

Boy: Where do fleas go in the winter?

Girl: Search me!

Boy scout: I'm in agony. I've been stung by a bee.
Scout leader: Well, we'll put some cream on it.
Boy scout: You'll be lucky, it must be miles away now.

Father: Why did you put a toad in your sister's bed?
Son: I couldn't find a spider.

Teacher: What did Robert the Bruce do after watching the spider climbing up and down?
Pupil: He went and invented the yo-yo.

Did you hear about the angry flea?
He was hopping mad.

Did you hear about the bloke who set up a flea circus?
He started it from scratch.

Did you hear about the religious moth?
He gave up woollens for lint.

Did you hear about the flea who failed his exams?
He didn't come up to scratch.

Did you hear about the boy who wanted to run away to the circus?
He ended up in a flea circus.

Knock, knock.
Who's there?
Weevil.
Weevil who?
Weevil work it out.

Knock, knock.
Who's there?
Flea.
Flea who?
Flea's a jolly good feller.

Knock, knock.
Who's there?
Flea.
Flea who?
Flea thirty!

Knock, knock.
Who's there?
Spider.
Spider who?
Spider through the keyhole.

Knock, knock.
Who's there?
Webster.
Webster who?
Webster Spin, your friendly
neighbourhood spider.

Knock, knock.
Who's there?
Mosquito.
Mosquito who?
Mosquito smoking soon.

Knock, knock.
Who's there?
Fly.
Fly who?
Fly away soon.

Knock, knock.
Who's there?
Moth.
Moth who?
Motht people know the anthwer.

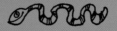

Knock, knock.
Who's there?
Earwig.
Earwig who?
Earwig come!

Knock, knock.
Who's there?
Grub.
Grub who?
Grub hold of my hand and let's go!

Knock, knock.
Who's there?
Roach.
Roach who?
Roach out and touch somebody.

Knock, knock.
Who's there?
Bee.
Bee who?
Bee careful out there!

Knock, knock.
Who's there?
Termite.
Termite who?
Termite's the night!

Knock, knock.
Who's there?
Army Ant.
Army Ant who?
Army Ants coming for tea, then?

Knock, knock.
Who's there?
Larva.
Larva who?
Larva cup of coffee.

Knock, knock.
Who's there?
Amos.
Amos who?
Amosquito.

Knock, knock.
Who's there?
Anna.
Anna who?
Annather mosquito.

Knock, knock.
Who's there?
Insect.
Insect who?
Insect your name and address
  here.

Knock, knock.
Who's there?
Bug.
Bug who?
Bugsy Malone.

Knock, knock.
Who's there?
Tristan.
Tristan who?
Tristan insect to really get up your
  nose.

Doctor, doctor, I keep seeing an insect spinning round.
Don't worry, it's just a bug that's going round.

Doctor, doctor, I keep thinking I'm a mosquito.
Go away, sucker.

Doctor, doctor, I keep thinking I'm a moth.
So why did you come to see me?
Well, I saw the light in the window . . .

Centipede: Doctor, doctor, when my feet hurt, I hurt all over.

Doctor, doctor, I keep thinking I'm a nit.
Oh, get out of my hair!

Doctor, doctor, I keep thinking I'm a bee.
Oh, buzz off!

Doctor, doctor, I keep thinking I'm a butterfly?
Will you say what you mean and stop flitting about?

Doctor, doctor, I keep thinking I'm a caterpillar.
Don't worry, you'll soon change.

Doctor, doctor, I keep thinking I'm a spider.
What a web of lies!

Doctor, doctor, I keep thinking I'm a moth.
Get out of the way, you're in my light.

Waiter, waiter! There's a fly in my soup.
What do you expect for two dollars, sir? A beetle?

Waiter, waiter! There's a flea in my soup.
Tell him to hop it.

Waiter, waiter! There's a fly in my soup!
Yes, sir, he's committed insecticide.

Waiter, waiter! There's a fly in my custard.
I'll fetch him a spoon, sir.

Waiter, waiter! There's a cockroach on my steak.
They don't seem to care what they eat, do they, sir?

Waiter, waiter! There's a maggot in my salad.
Don't worry, he won't live long in that stuff.

Waiter, waiter! There's a spider in my soup.
It's hardly deep enough to drown him, sir.

Waiter, waiter! There's a wasp in my pudding.
So that's where they go to in the winter.

Waiter, waiter! There's a dead spider in my soup.
Yes, madam, they can't stand the boiling water.

Waiter, waiter! There's a fly in my soup.
Yes, that's the manager, sir. The last customer was a witch doctor.

Waiter, waiter! There's a fly in my wine.
Well, you did ask for something with a little body, sir.

Waiter, waiter! There's a fly in my soup.
Yes, madam, it's the bad meat that attracts them.

Waiter, waiter! What's this dead fly doing on my meat?
I don't know, madam, it must have died after tasting it.

Waiter, waiter! There's a spider in my soup. Send for the manager! It's no good, sir, he's frightened of them too.

Waiter, waiter! What's this spider doing in my alphabet soup?
Probably learning to read, sir.

Waiter, waiter! There's a beetle in my soup.
Sorry, sir, we're out of flies today.

Waiter, waiter! What's this fly doing in my soup?
The butterfly stroke by the look of it, sir.

Waiter, waiter! There's a mosquito in my soup.
Don't worry, sir, mosquitoes have very small appetites.

Waiter, waiter! There's a fly in my soup.
Not fussy what they eat, are they, sir?

Waiter, waiter! There's a dead fly in my soup.
Yes, sir, it's the heat that kills them.

Waiter, waiter! There's a fly in the butter.
Yes, sir, it's a butterfly.

Waiter, waiter! There's a fly in my soup.
Don't panic, sir. I'll call the RSPCA.

Waiter, waiter! There's a fly in my soup!
Don't worry, sir, the spider in your bread will get it.

Waiter, waiter! There's a bee in my alphabet soup.
Yes, sir, and I hope there's an A, a C and all the other letters too.

Waiter, waiter! There are two flies in my soup.
That's all right, sir. Have the extra one on me.

Waiter, waiter! What's this spider doing in my soup?
Trying to save the fly from drowning by the look of it, sir.

Waiter, waiter! There's a spider in my salad.
Yes, sir, the chef's using Webb lettuces today.

Waiter, waiter, what's this cockroach doing on my ice-cream sundae?
I think it's skiing downhill.

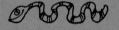

Waiter, waiter, there's a fly in my soup.
Just a minute, sir, I'll get the fly spray.

What kind of ant is good at adding up?
An account-ant.

What medicine do you give a sick ant?
Antibiotics.

What do you call an ant with five
pairs of eyes?
Ant-ten-eye.

Who is the most royal ant?
Princess Ant.

Why did the ant-elope?
Nobody gnu.

What's worse than ants in your pants?
A bat in your bra.

What kind of ant can you color with?
A cray-ant.

What game do ants play with monsters?
Squash.

What do you call an ant who can't play the piano?
Discord-ant.

What do you get if you cross an ant with half a pair of knickers?
Pant.

What do you call an ant that likes to be alone?
An Independ-ant.

What do you call an ant with frog's legs?
An ant-phibian.

If ants are such busy insects, how come they find the time to turn up to picnics?

What do you call an eighty-year-old ant?
An antique.

Why don't anteaters get sick?
Because they're full of anty-
bodies!

Who was the most famous French
ant?
Napoleant.

What's the biggest ant in the
world?
An eleph-ant.

What is even bigger than that?
A Gi-ant.

What do you call an ant who lives
with your great-uncle?
Your great-ant.

What is smaller than an ant's
dinner?
An ant's mouth.

How many ants are needed to fill
an apartment?
Ten-ants.

Who was the most famous
scientist ant?
Albert Antstein.

Where do ants eat?
In a restaur-ant.

What do you call ant space
travelers?
Cosmon-ants.

What do you call a smart ant?
Eleg-ant.

What kind of ants are very
learned?
Ped-ants.

What do you call a foreign ant?
Import-ant.

Where do ants go for their
holidays?
Fr-ants.

What do you call a greedy ant?
An anteater.

What do you call a scruffy, lazy ant?
Decad-ant.

What do you get if you cross some ants with some tics?
All sorts of antics.

What do you call an ant who honestly hates school?
A tru-ant.

What has fifty legs but can't walk?
Half a centipede.

Why did the insects drop the centipede from their football team?
It took him so long to put his boots on.

Why do centipedes make such poor footballers?
By the time they put their boots on, the match is nearly over.

What's worse than a giraffe with a sore throat?
A centipede with chilblains.

What goes ninety-nine clonk, ninety-nine clonk?
A centipede with a wooden leg.

Centipede to pal: I just hate it when I start the day off on the wrong foot.

What do you call a guard with 100 legs?
A sentrypede.

Why was the centipede late?
Because she was playing This Little Piggy with her baby.

What do you get if you cross a centipede with a parrot?
A walkie-talkie.

What is worse than a crocodile with toothache?
A centipede with athlete's foot.

What do you get if you cross a centipede with a chicken?
Enough drumsticks for an army.

What did one centipede say to another?
You've got a lovely pair of legs, pair of legs, pair of legs...

What has 100 legs and goes in one ear and out the other?
A centipede in a corn field
(geddit?)

What kind of wig can hear?
An earwig.

What did the earwig say when it fell down the stairs?
Ear we go!

Why don't the other insects like earwigs?
Because they're always earwigging their conversations.

What do you get if you cross a tarantula with a rose?
I don't know but I wouldn't try smelling one.

What happened when the chef found a daddy-long-legs in the lettuce?
The insect became daddy-short-legs.

Why did the spider buy a car?
He wanted to take it out for a spin.

What's red and dangerous?
Raspberry and tarantula jelly.

What did the spiders say to the fly?
We're getting married. Do you want to come to the webbing?

What did Mrs Spider say to Mr Spider when he broke her new web?
Darn it!

What does a spider do when he gets angry?
He goes up the wall.

How do you know if a spider is with it?
He doesn't have a web, he has a website.

What are spiders' webs good for?
Spiders.

Why do spiders enjoy swimming?
They have webbed feet.

What's a spider's favorite TV
show?
The Newly-Web Game.

What do you call a big Irish spider?
Paddy-long-legs.

What would happen if tarantulas
were as big as horses?
If one bit you, you could ride it to
hospital.

Why are spiders like tops?
They're always spinning.

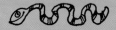

Where do spiders go for fun?
To Webley.

What has eight legs and likes
living in trees?
Four anti-road protestors.

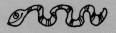

What kind of doctors are spiders like?
Spin doctors.

What do you call a hundred spiders on a tire?
A spinning wheel.

What did Mrs Spider say to Mr Spider when he explained why he was home late?
You're spinning me a yarn.

What pillar doesn't hold a building
up?
A caterpillar.

What does a cat go to sleep on?
A caterpillar.

What's green and dangerous?
A caterpillar with a hand-grenade.

What does a caterpillar do on New Year's Day?
Turns over a new leaf.

What is a grasshopper?
An insect on a pogo stick.

What's the definition of a caterpillar?
A worm in a fur coat.

What is green and sooty and whistles when it rubs its back legs together?
Chimney Cricket.

What is green and can jump a mile a minute?
A grasshopper with hiccoughs.

What do you call a grasshopper
with no legs?
A grass-hovver.

Why is it better to be a grasshopper
than a cricket?
Because grasshoppers can play
cricket but there's no such game
as grasshopper.

What do you call a flea that lives in
an idiot's ear?
A space invader.

What do you get if you cross a flea with a rabbit?
A bug's bunny.

How do you start an insect race?
One, two, flea, go!

What's the difference between a flea and a coyote?
One prowls on the hairy, the other howls on the prairie.

What did the clean dog say to the insect?
Long time, no flea!

What's a flea's favorite science fiction book?
The Itch-hiker's Guide to the Galaxy.

What do you call a flea that lives in Russia?
A Moscow-ito.

How do you find out where a flea
has bitten you?
Start from scratch.

Why did the stupid boy wear a
turtleneck sweater?
To hide his flea collar.

What's the difference between
fleas and dogs?
Dogs can have fleas but fleas
can't have dogs.

Why was the mother flea feeling
down in the dumps?
Because she thought her children
were all going to the dogs.

Who rides a dog and was a
Confederate general during the
American Civil War?
Robert E. Flea.

What did the idiot do to the flea in
his ear?
Shot it!

What did one flea say to another after a night out?
Shall we walk home or take a dog?

Two fleas were running across the top of a packet of soap powder.
"Why are we running so fast?" gasped one.
"Because it says, 'Tear Along the Dotted Line'."

What is the most faithful insect on the planet?
Fleas. Once they find someone they like they stick to them.

If a flea and a fly pass each other, what time is it?
Fly past flea.

How do fleas travel?
Itch hiking.

What do you call a cheerful flea?
A hop-timist.

What insect runs away from
everything?
A flee.

Waiter, waiter! There's a dead fly in
my soup.
Oh no! Who's going to look after
his family?

Waiter, waiter! What's this creepy crawly thing doing in my lettuce? I think he's trying to get out, madam.

Waiter, waiter! What's this creepy crawly thing doing in my dinner? Oh, that one – he comes here every night.

Waiter, waiter! What's this creepy crawly thing doing waltzing round my table?
It's the band, sir, it's playing his tune.

Waiter, waiter! What's this creepy crawly thing doing on my wife's shoulder?
I don't know – friendly thing, isn't he?

Waiter, waiter! There's a fly in my starter. Get rid of it, would you?
I can't do that, sir, he hasn't had his main course yet.

Waiter, waiter! There's a teeny beetle in my broccoli.
I'll see if I can find a bigger one, madam.

Waiter, waiter! There's a fly in my soup.
Go ahead and eat him. There are plenty more where he came from.

Sir, you haven't touched your custard.
No, I'm waiting for the fly to stop using it as a trampoline.

Waiter, waiter, what's this fly doing on my ice-cream?
Looks like he's learning to ski, sir.

Waiter, waiter! There's a fly in my soup!
Just wait until you see the main course.

Waiter, waiter! There's a dead fly swimming in my soup.
Nonsense, sir, dead flies can't swim.

Waiter, waiter! There's a fly in my soup?
And what's the problem, sir?
I ordered slug soup.

Waiter, waiter! What kind of insect is this I've found in my dinner?
I don't know, sir, I can't tell one breed from another.

Waiter, waiter! There's a fly in my bean soup.
Don't worry, sir, I'll take it back and exchange it for a bean.

Waiter, waiter! What's this fly doing in my ice-cream?
Maybe he likes winter sports.

Waiter, waiter! What's this fly doing in my soup?
I think it's drowning, sir.

Why do waiters prefer monsters to flies?
Have you ever heard anyone complaining of a monster in their soup?

Two ants were watching a useless golfer swing wildly, trying to hit the ball. One said to the other, "Come on, lets get on the ball before he hits us."

Two mosquitoes were buzzing round when they saw a drunken man. One said to the other, "You bite him – I'm driving."

A flea jumped over the swinging doors of a saloon, drank three whiskeys and jumped out again. He picked himself up from the dirt, dusted himself down and said, "OK, who moved my dog?"

Elephants

What do you get if you cross a
jellyfish with an elephant?
Jelly the Elephant.

What do you get if you cross an
elephant with some locusts?
I'm not sure, but if they ever swarm
– watch out!

What do you get if you cross a
worm with an elephant?
Big holes in your garden.

Why do elephants have trunks?
Because they don't have glove
compartments.

Why doesn't Kermit like
elephants?
They always want to play leap-frog
with him.

How can you prevent an elephant
from charging?
Take away his credit card.

Tom: What did the banana say to the elephant?
Nik: I don't know.
Tom: Nothing. Bananas can't talk.

What is Smokey the Elephant's middle name?
The.

Why did the elephant put his trunk across the trail?
To trip up the ants.

What do you get if you cross an elephant with a spider?
I don't know but if it crawled over your ceiling the house would collapse.

A cannibal was walking through the jungle when he came to a clearing and saw a freshly killed elephant lying down with a pigmy standing on top of it, brandishing a big stick and doing a victory dance. "Have you just killed that elephant?" asked the cannibal. "Yes," replied the pigmy, "I did it with my club."

"Wow," said the cannibal, "you must have a really big club!"

"Yes," replied the pigmy, "there are about forty of us in it!"

What do you get if you cross an elephant with the abominable snowman?
A jumbo yeti.

Reports are coming in of an elephant doing a ton in the highway. Police ask motorists to drive carefully and to treat it as a roundabout.

What's the best thing to give a seasick elephant?
Plenty of room.

Why did the elephant paint her head yellow?
To see if blondes really do have more fun.

Anna: I was top of the class last week.

Mom: How did you manage that?

Anna: I managed to answer a question about elephants.

Mom: What question?

Anna: Well, the teacher asked us how many legs an elephant had, and I said five.

Mom: But that wasn't right.

Anna: I know, but it was the nearest anyone got.

Which animals were the last to leave the ark?
The elephants – they were packing their trunks.

What do you get if you cross a caretaker with an elephant?
A 20-ton school cleaner.

My dad is so short-sighted he can't get to sleep unless he counts elephants.

How do you get an elephant into a car?
Open the door.

Farm Animals

What do you get if you cross a
worm with a young goat?
A dirty kid.

Waiter, this food isn't fit for a pig!
All right, I'll get you some that is.

What do you get if you cross a
snake with a pig?
A boar constrictor.

What do you get if you cross a
monster with a cow and an oat
field?
Lumpy porridge.

What happened to the vampire who
swallowed a sheep?
He felt baaaaaaaaaaaaad.

Visitor: Wow, you have a lot of flies buzzing round your horses and cows. Do you ever shoo them?
Rancher: No, we just let them go barefoot.

Joe: Did you ever see a horse fly?
Pete: No, but I once saw a cow jump off a cliff.

"I told you to draw a picture of a cow eating grass," said the art master. "Why have you handed in a blank sheet of paper?"

"Because the cow ate all the grass, that's why there's no grass."

"But what about the cow?"

"There wasn't much point in it hanging around when there was nothing to eat, so he went back to the barn."

"I asked you to draw a pony and trap," said the art master. "You've only drawn the pony. Why?"

"Well, sir. I thought the pony would draw the trap."

"What did the doctor say to you yesterday?" asked the teacher.

"He said I was allergic to horses."

"I've never heard of anyone suffering from that. What's the condition called?"

"Bronco-itis."

The teacher was furious with her son. "Just because you've been put in my class, there's no need to think you can take liberties. You're a pig." The boy said nothing. "Well! Do you know what a pig is?"
"Yes, Mom," said the boy. "The offspring of a swine."

Why should a school not be near a chicken farm?
To avoid the pupils overhearing fowl language.

An idiot decided to start a chicken farm so he bought a hundred chickens. A month later he returned to the dealer for another hundred chickens because all of the first lot had died. A month later he was back at the dealer's for another hundred chickens for the second lot had also died. "But I think I know where I'm going wrong," said the idiot, "I think I'm planting them too deep."

What's a sheep's hairdresser
called?
A baa-baa shop.

Did you hear about the idiot who made his chickens drink boiling water?
He thought they would lay hard-boiled eggs.

What happened when the ghostly cows got out of their field?
There was udder chaos.

What does a headless horseman ride?
A nightmare.

Mary had a bionic cow,
It lived on safety pins.
And every time she milked that
   cow,
The milk came out in tins.

On which side does a chicken
have the most feathers?
On the outside.

Two friends who lived in the town were chatting. "I've just bought a pig," said the first.

"But where will you keep it?" said the second. "Your garden's much too small for a pig!"

"I'm going to keep it under my bed," replied his friend.

"But what about the smell?

"He'll soon get used to that."

The Stock Market is a place where sheep and cattle are sold.

Dad, that Mr Jenkins down the road said you weren't fit to live with pigs!

What did you say, son?

I stuck up for you. I said you were certainly fit to live with pigs.

What did the neurotic pig say to the farmer?

You take me for grunted.

Doctor, doctor, I've got a little sty.
Then you'd better buy a little pig.

Dim Dinah wrote in her exercise
book: Margarine is butter made
from imitation cows.

How do phantom hens dance?
Chick to chick.

Fish and Sea Creatures

Why did the slippery eel blush?
Because the sea weed.

What goes straight up in the air
and wobbles?
A jellyfishcopter.

How do you start a jellyfish race?
Get set!

What do you get if you cross an octopus with a skunk?
An octopong.

How did the octopus lovers walk down the road?
Arm in arm in arm in arm in arm in arm in arm in arm.

What do you get if you cross a jellyfish with a sheepdog?
Colliewobbles.

What did the octopus say to his moneylender?
Here's the sick squid I owe you.

What do octopuses play in their spare time?
Name that tuna.

What do you call a neurotic octopus?
A crazy, mixed-up squid.

What does an octopus wear when
it's cold?
A coat of arms.

What do you get if you cross a
bottle of water with an electric
eel?
A bit of a shock really!

What do you get if you cross an eel
with a shopper?
A slippery customer.

What's slimy, tastes of raspberry
and wobbly and lives in the sea?
A red jellyfish.

What do you get if you cross a
jellyfish with an elephant?
Jelly the Elephant.

What is wobbly, slimy and white
with red spots?
A jellyfish with measles.

One goldfish to his tankmate: If there's no god, who changes the water?

Why did the jellyfish's wife leave him?
He stung her into action.

What do you get if you cross an electric eel and a sponge?
Shock absorbers.

What did the jellyfish say when she saw the electric eel?
How shocking!

How do eels get around the
seabed?
They go by octobus.

What's wet and wiggly and says
"How do you do" sixteen times?
Two octopuses shaking hands.

What is an eel's favorite song?
Slip Sliding Away.

Have you heard the joke about the slippery eel?
You wouldn't grasp it.

What is a sea monster's favorite dish?
Fish and ships.

What did the Loch Ness Monster say to his friend?
Long time, no sea.

What is an octopus?
An eight-sided cat.

There once was a lonely young
   jellyfish.
Who then met a sweet, loving
   shellyfish.
They went with the motion
Of waves in the ocean.
And became better known as the
   jollyfish.

Girl: Do you know what family the octopus belongs to?
Boy: No one in our street.

Did you hear about the man who tried to cross the Loch Ness Monster with a goat?
He had to get a new goat.

Did you hear about the stupid jellyfish?
It set!

Knock, knock.
Who's there?
Eel.
Eel who?
Eel meet again.

Doctor, doctor, I feel like an electric eel.
That's shocking.

What happened when one jellyfish met another?
They produced jelly babies.

One day, a boy was walking down the street when he saw a sea monster standing on the corner looking lost. The boy put a lead on the sea monster and took him to the police station. "You should take him to the museum," said the police sergeant.

The next day the police sergeant saw the boy in the town still with the monster on a lead. "I thought I told you to take him to the museum," said the policeman.

"I did," said the boy, "and today I'm taking him to the movies."

What do you get if you cross the
Loch Ness Monster with a shark?
Loch Jaws.

What eats its victims two by two?
Noah's Shark.

How do you communicate with the
Loch Ness Monster at 20,000
fathoms?
Drop him a line.

What fish tastes best with cream?
A jellyfish.

Teacher: Martin, put some more water in the fish tank.
Martin: But, sir, they haven't drunk the water I gave them yesterday.

What sort of fish performs surgical operations?
A sturgeon.

Mrs Turbot, the biology teacher, was very fond of fish. She was also rather deaf, which was great for the children in her class. What Mrs Turbot needs, said one of her colleagues, is a herring-aid.

The vampire went into the Monster Cafe. "Shark and chips," he ordered. "And make it snappy."

Pets

Why is a frog luckier than a cat?
Because a frog croaks all the time
– a cat only croaks nine times.

What would you get if you crossed
a frog with a little dog?
A croaker spaniel.

What is the definition of a narrow
squeak?
A thin mouse.

What goes eek, eek, bang?
A mouse in a minefield.

What's grey and squeaky and
hangs around in caves?
Stalagmice.

What's the hardest part about
milking a mouse?
Getting the bucket underneath it.

Who is the king of all the mice?
Mouse Tse Tung.

What do angry rodents send each
other at Christmas?
Cross mouse cards.

Which mouse was a Roman
emperor?
Julius Cheeser.

Hickory, dickory, dock,
The mice ran up the clock.
The clock struck one,
And the rest got away with minor
  injuries.

What is grey and hairy and lives on
a man's face?
A mousetache.

What's grey and furry on the
inside and white on the outside?
A mouse sandwich.

What do you call a mouse that can pick up a monster?
Sir.

How do mice celebrate when they move house?
With a mouse-warming party.

What did the mouse say when his friend broke his front teeth?
Hard cheese.

Why did the mouse eat a candle?
For light refreshment.

What is a mouse's favorite game?
Hide and squeak.

What goes "dot, dot, dash, squeak"?
Mouse code.

What is white one minute and
brown the next?
A rat in a microwave oven.

Who has large antlers, has a high
voice and wears white gloves?
Mickey Moose.

What is brown one minute and white the next?
A rat in a deep-freeze.

What do you get if you cross a mouse with a packet of soap powder?
Bubble and Squeak.

Which Cornish town is the favorite
holiday spot for rodents?
Mousehole.

What is small, furry and smells like
bacon?
A hamster.

Why do mice need oiling?
Because they squeak.

What is a mouse's favorite record?
Please cheese me.

What's a rat's least favorite
record?
What's up, Pussycat?

How do you save a drowning
rodent?
Use mouse-to-mouse
resuscitation.

What kind of musical instrument
do rats play?
Mouse organ.

How can you tell the difference
between a rabbit and a red-eyed
monster?
Just try getting a red-eyed
monster into a rabbit hutch.

Why was the Abominable
Snowman's dog called Frost?
Because Frost bites.

What has six legs and flies?
A witch giving her cat a lift.

Why are black cats such good singers?
They're very mewsical.

When it is unlucky to see a black cat?
When you're a mouse.

What do you call it when a witch's cat falls off her broomstick?
A catastrophe.

What do you get if you cross a witch's cat with Father Christmas?
Santa Claws.

How do you get milk from a witch's cat?
Steal her saucer.

What do you get if you cross a
witch's cat with a canary?
A peeping tom.

Why did the witch feed her cat
with pennies?
She wanted to put them in the
kitty.

What do witches' cats eat for
breakfast?
Mice Krispies.

Why do black cats never shave?
Because eight out of ten cats
prefer Whiskas.

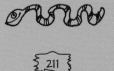

Why is a witch's kitten like an unhealed wound?
Both are a little pussy.

What do you call a witch's cat that drinks vinegar?
A sour puss.

What do you call a witch's cat who never comes when she's called?
Im-puss-able.

Now you see it . . . now you don't –
What are you looking at?
A black cat walking over a zebra
crossing.

What has four legs, a tail, whiskers
and flies?
A dead witch's cat.

What has four legs, a tail, whiskers
and goes round and round for
hours?
A black cat in a tumble-drier.

What has four legs, a tail, whiskers
and cuts grass?
A lawn miaower.

What do you get if you cross a
witch's cat and a canary?
A cat with a full tummy.

What do you call a witch's cat with
no legs?
Anything you like – she won't be
able to come anyway.

What is a black cat's favorite TV
program?
Miami Mice.

What's furry, has whiskers and
chases outlaws?
A posse cat.

Ding, dong, bell,
Pussy's down the well,
But we've put some disinfectant
  down
And don't mind about the smell.

What do witches' cats strive for?
Purr-fection.

What do you call a witch's cat who can spring from the ground to her mistress's hat in one leap?
A good jum-purr.

What do you call a witch's cat who can do spells as well as her mistress?
An ex-purr-t.

What is pink, has a curly tail and
drinks blood?
A hampire.

Why did the skeleton run up a
tree?
Because a dog was after its
bones.

What did Dr. Frankenstein get
when he put his goldfish's brain in
the body of his dog?
I don't know, but it is great at
chasing submarines.

There once was a very strong cat
Who had a fight with a bat.
The bat flew away
And at the end of the day
The cat had a scrap with a rat.

What's white, fluffy and floats?
A cat-emeringue.

Mother: Keep that dog out of the house, it's full of fleas.
Son: Keep out of the house, Fido, it's full of fleas.

Wizard: Have you put the cat out?
Witch: Was he burning again?

Customer: I'd like a moustrap, please.

Assistant: Have you tried Boots?

Customer: I'd like to catch it, not kick it to death.

1st Witch: My boyfriend's gone and stolen my black cat.

2nd Witch: You mean your familiar.

1st Witch: Well, we were, but I'm not speaking to him now.

Witch: Doctor, doctor, I keep thinking I'm my own cat.
Doctor: How long have you thought this?
Witch: Since I was a kitten.

Emm: What's the name of your dog?
Nik: Ginger.
Emm: Does Ginger bite?
Nik: No, but Ginger snaps.

What's gor four legs, barks and goes "tick tock"?
A watch dog.

What's furry, has whiskers and chases outlaws?
A posse cat.

What's the difference between a flea-bitten dog and a bored visitor?
One's going to itch. The other's itching to go.

A workman had just finished laying a carpet in a witch's house when he realised he had lost his sandwiches. Looking round he saw a lump under the carpet. Not wanting to pull the carpet up again he just got a bit plank of wood and smashed the lump flat. Then the witch came into the room with a cup of tea for him. "Here's your tea," she said. "My, you've laid the carpet well. Just one thing, though, have you seen my pet toad anywhere?"

A wizard went to the doctor one day complaining of headaches. "It's because I live in the same room as two of my brothers," he said. "One of them has six goats and the other has four pigs and they all live in the room with us. The smell is terrible.

"Well, couldn't you just open the windows," asked the doctor.

"Certainly not," he replied, "my bats would fly out."

"Won't you let me live one of my own lives?' said the put-upon young cat to its parents.

A blind rabbit and a blind snake ran into each other on the road one day. The snake reached out, touched the rabbit and said, "You're soft and fuzzy and have floppy ears. You must be a rabbit." The rabbit reached out, touched the snake and said, "You're slimy, beady-eyed and low to the ground. You must be a maths teacher."

Why did a man's pet vulture not
make a sound for five years?
It was stuffed.

What happened to the skeleton
that was attacked by a dog?
The dog ran off with some bones
and left him without a leg to stand
on.

What did one black cat say to the other?
Nothing. Cats can't speak.

What did the black cat do when its tail was cut off?
It went to a re-tail store.

What do you get when a vampire bites a rat?
A neighborhood free of cats.

Two monsters went duck-hunting with their dogs but without success. "I know what we're doing wrong," said the first one.
"What's that then?" said the second.
"We're not throwing the dogs high enough!"

"Mary," said her teacher, "you can't bring that lamb into school. What about the smell?"
"Oh, that's all right, Miss," said Mary. "It'll soon get used to it."

Mouse I: I've trained that crazy science teacher at last.

Mouse II: How have you done that?

Mouse I: I don't know how, but every time I run through that maze and ring the bell, he gives me a piece of cheese.

It's obvious that animals are smarter than humans. Put eight horses in a race and 20,000 people will go along to see it. But put eight people in a race and not one horse will bother to go along and watch.

Jim: Our dog is just like one of the family.
Fred: Which one?

There was once a puppy called May who loved to pick quarrels with animals who were bigger than she was. One day she argued with a lion. The next day was the first of June. Why? Because that was the end of May!

What kind of cats love water?
Octopusses.

My dog saw a sign that said: Wet
Paint – so he did!

My dog is a nuisance. He chases
everyone on a bicycle. What can I
do?
Take his bike away.

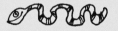

What's an American cat's favorite car?
A Catillac.

A man went into the local department store where he saw a sign on the escalator – Dogs must be carried on this escalator. The man then spent the next two hours looking for a dog.

How does an idiot call for his dog?
He puts two fingers in his mouth
and then shouts "Rover".

"I'm sorry to call you out at this
time of night," said the witch, "but
it's my poor black cat. He's just
lying there telling me he wants to
die."
The monster vet licked his lips.
"Well, you've done the right thing
by sending for me."

Teacher: And did you see the Catskill Mountains on your visit to America?

Jimmy: No, but I saw them kill mice.

A motorist approached the principal one afternoon and said, "I'm awfully sorry, but I think I've just run over the school cat. Can I replace it?"

The principal looked him up and down and replied, "I doubt if you'd be the mouser she was."

What do you get if you pour hot
water down a rabbit hole?
Hot cross bunnies!

What's a twip?
What a wabbit calls a twain ride!

What happened when the
headmistress's poodle swallowed
a roll of film?
Nothing serious developed.

A man out for a walk came across a little boy pulling his cat's tail. "Hey, you!" he called. "Don't pull the cat's tail!"

"I'm not pulling!" replied the little boy. "I'm only holding on – the cat's doing the pulling!"

What happened when the pussy swallowed a penny? There was money in the kitty.

Did you hear about the witch who fed her pet vulture on sawdust? The vulture laid ten eggs and when they hatched, nine chicks had wooden legs and the tenth was a woodpecker.

Caspar: I was the teacher's pet last year.
Jaspar: Why was that?
Caspar: She couldn't afford a dog.

What do ghosts like about riding horses?
Ghoulloping.

Wild Animals

What do you get if you cross a bee with a skunk?
A creature that stinks and stings.

How can you tell if a Yeti's been in the fridge?
There are paw prints in the trifle.

What kind of money do yetis use?
Iced lolly.

What exams do Yetis take?
Snow levels.

What do you get if you cross a giant, hairy monster with a penguin?
I don't know but it's in a very tight-fitting dinner suit.

What happened to the cannibal lion?
He had to swallow his pride.

Boy: I once met a lion who had
been bitten by a snake.
Girl: What did he say?
Boy: Nothing, silly, lions don't talk!

"It's cruel," said the papa bear to
his family on seeing a car load of
humans, "to keep them caged up
like that."

A man in a movie theater notices what looks like a bear sitting next to him.

"Are you a bear?"

"Yes."

"What are you doing at the movies?"

"Well, I liked the book."

What do you get if you cross a porcupine with a giraffe?
A long-necked toothbrush.

What's a porcupine's favorite food?
Prickled onions.

How do you catch a squirrel?
Climb up a tree and act like a nut.

What should you do if you find a
gorilla sitting at your school desk?
Sit somewhere else.

What did the stupid ghost call his pet tiger?
Spot.

Why was the mother kangaroo cross with her children?
Because they ate crisps in bed.

Baby Skunk: But, Mom, why can't I have a chemistry set for my birthday?
Mother: Because it would stink the house out, that's why.

What's black and white and makes
a lot of noise?
A zebra with a set of drums.

What do you call a deer with no eyes?
No idea.

How many skunks does it take to make a big stink?
A phew!

Why do giraffes have such long legs?
Because they have smelly feet.